On the WING

North American Birds 3

Andrea Voon

Richard Han

← 45cm →

Mourning Dove

French: Tourterelle triste

Little wings, little wings, flap flap flap...

Peacemakers in the open woodlands are on the wing.

Mourning Doves, Mourning Doves, clap clap clap...

Bring hope in hard times as they sing.

koo-KOO-kook

← 40cm →

American Robin

French: Merle d'Amérique

Little wings, little wings, flap flap flap…

Cheerleaders in the open woodlands are on the wing.

American Robins, American Robins, clap clap clap…

Spring is in the air as they sing.

cheerily… cheer-up… cheer-up…

Downy Woodpecker

French: Pic mineur

← 30cm →

Little wings, little wings, flap flap flap…

Drummers in the forests are on the wing.

Downy Woodpeckers, Downy Woodpeckers, clap clap clap…

Drum against wood and metal as they sing.

Fox Sparrow
French: Bruant fauve

←29cm→

Little wings, little wings, flap flap flap…

Traffic officers in the forests are on the wing.

Fox Sparrows, Fox Sparrows, clap clap clap…

Spot their chevron markings as they sing.

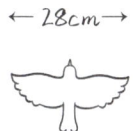

← 28cm →

Spotted Towhee

French: Tohi tacheté

Little wings, little wings, flap flap flap...

Tea masters in the scrubs are on the wing.

Spotted Towhees, Spotted Towhees, clap clap clap...

Hop and scratch on leaves as they sing.

Drink-your-teeeeea-

drink-drink-your-teeea-

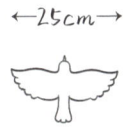

←25cm→

Golden-crowned Sparrow

French: Bruant à couronne dorée

Little wings, little wings, flap flap flap...

Gold miners in the scrubs are on the wing.

Golden-crowned Sparrows, Golden-crowned Sparrows, clap clap clap...

Tears will flood the earth as they sing.

I'm-so-tired~~

Oh-dear-me

no-gold-hereee~

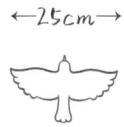

←25cm→

House Sparrow

French: Moineau domestique

Little wings, little wings, flap flap flap...

Housekeepers in the towns are on the wing.

House Sparrows, House Sparrows, clap clap clap...

Enjoy a dust bath as they sing.

Dark-eyed Junco

French: Junco ardoisé

←25cm→

Little wings, little wings, flap flap flap...

Mountain guides in the forests are on the wing.

Dark-eyed Juncos, Dark-eyed Juncos, clap clap clap...

Snow is falling as they sing.

Song Sparrow

French: Bruant chanteur

←24cm→

Little wings, little wings, flap flap flap…

Disc jockeys in the open woodlands are on the wing.

Song Sparrows, Song Sparrows, clap clap clap…

Shuffle their song list as they sing.

White-crowned Sparrow
French: Bruant à couronne blanche

← 24cm →

Little wings, little wings, flap flap flap…

Translators in the scrubs are on the wing.

White-crowned Sparrows, white-crowned Sparrows, clap clap clap…

Learn a local dialect as they sing.

Savannah Sparrow

French: Bruant des prés

Little wings, little wings, flap flap flap...

Makeup artists in the grasslands are on the wing.

Savannah Sparrows, Savannah Sparrows, clap clap clap...

Apply yellow eyeshadow as they sing.

←15cm→

Marsh Wren
French: Troglodyte des marais

Tiny wings, tiny wings, flap flap flap…

Sword fighters in the marshes are on the wing.

Marsh Wrens, Marsh Wrens, clap clap clap…

Stay down and bounce secretly as they sing.

Little wings, tiny wings, flap flap flap...

Nesting Mama birds are on the wing.

Little wings, tiny wings, clap clap clap...

Blend into their surroundings as they sing.

Author

Andrea Voon

Over the past few years, Andrea has learned and grown with her family as a full-time mother in Canada. Back in Malaysia, she was a Chinese immersion elementary school teacher. In 2021, Andrea started her journey as an author. Growing up in a multilingual environment, Andrea loves the beauty of languages on their own. She has the vision to publish picture books to support bilingual families in raising their children in English, Chinese, and Cantonese reading.

Photographer

Richard Han

Richard loves to practice patience through his lenses of the natural world. He enjoys observing the wildlife and photographing the natural lifestyles that animals live. He is excited to present the beautiful photos that he captured in dreamy tones and colors to all the birds lover.

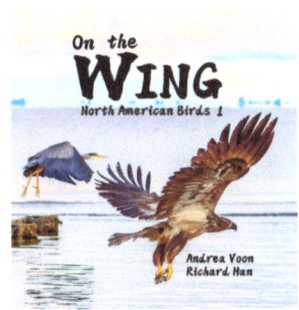

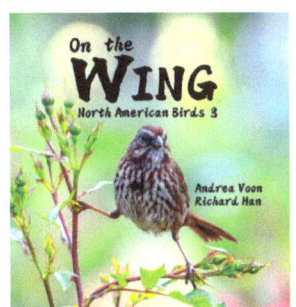
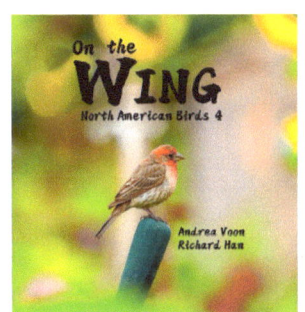

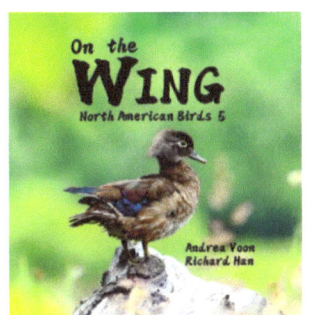

To **Shirley Han, Derek, Eliana, Alayna & Magnus Dominus**

with love -- Andrea. V

For **Richard Han**

The patience in natural photography

ISBN 978-1-998856-47-3
Text Copyright © 2024 Andrea Voon
Photo Credit © 2024 Richard Han